A note to teachers

The concepts in these colouring pages cover a wide range of learning levels ... many students to know *all* of them. I hope you'll use this book as more of an exploratory tool than a "test" or "check-up" on what students already know. Even if your student doesn't know the word *accelerando* when they finish colouring the sheet, it's sure to sound familiar the next time they hear it.

Musical Hues would be perfect to keep in the waiting room at your studio, to give to siblings when they're sitting in on a lesson or to send home over teaching breaks. Encourage your student to try and guess what the abstracted instrument is before and after they colour it in. Look up the instrument to see what it sounds like too!

A note to colourers

You may come across music symbols, notes and marks that you don't know yet in the course of colouring this book. That's totally fine – you can't know everything! I encourage you to look these up as you go and find out a bit about them. Ask your teacher or parent if you're not sure exactly what the definitions mean.

You might also come across some colours you've never heard of (maroon, anyone?). I've been quite descriptive and specific with the colour names so that your creations can really come to life when you're done. If there's a colour you don't have on hand, you can always make it with a bit of experimentation. For example, if you look up maroon and learn that it's a sort of red-purple colour, try colouring lightly with red first and then going over it with purple. If the instructions call for 3 shades of grey but you only have 2, you can create a third by colouring very gently for the lighter shade and more heavily for the darker shade.

And, finally, a note about your tools. I recommend using either colouring pencils or crayons, rather than markers. If you are going to use markers, make sure to put a spare rough sheet of paper underneath the page you're colouring so that it doesn't bleed through and accidentally colour in the page behind it.

A note about me

If you're reading this in certain parts of the world, you may have noticed one thing about me already: I spell the word "colour" wrong. No, it's not a typo. It's because I live in Ireland and that's how we spell it here – promise!

Aside from spending my time putting "U"s back where they belong, I teach piano to delightful children and adults in my home studio in Dublin. I also run a site called *Vibrant Music Teaching* that helps other music teachers and their students have more fun while learning about music together through creative resources and games.

I really hope you enjoy this book and I would simply love to see your colourful creations when they're done. Post a photo on Facebook or Instagram and tag me @ColourfulKeys so I can see how you put your own creative stamp on it. Have fun!

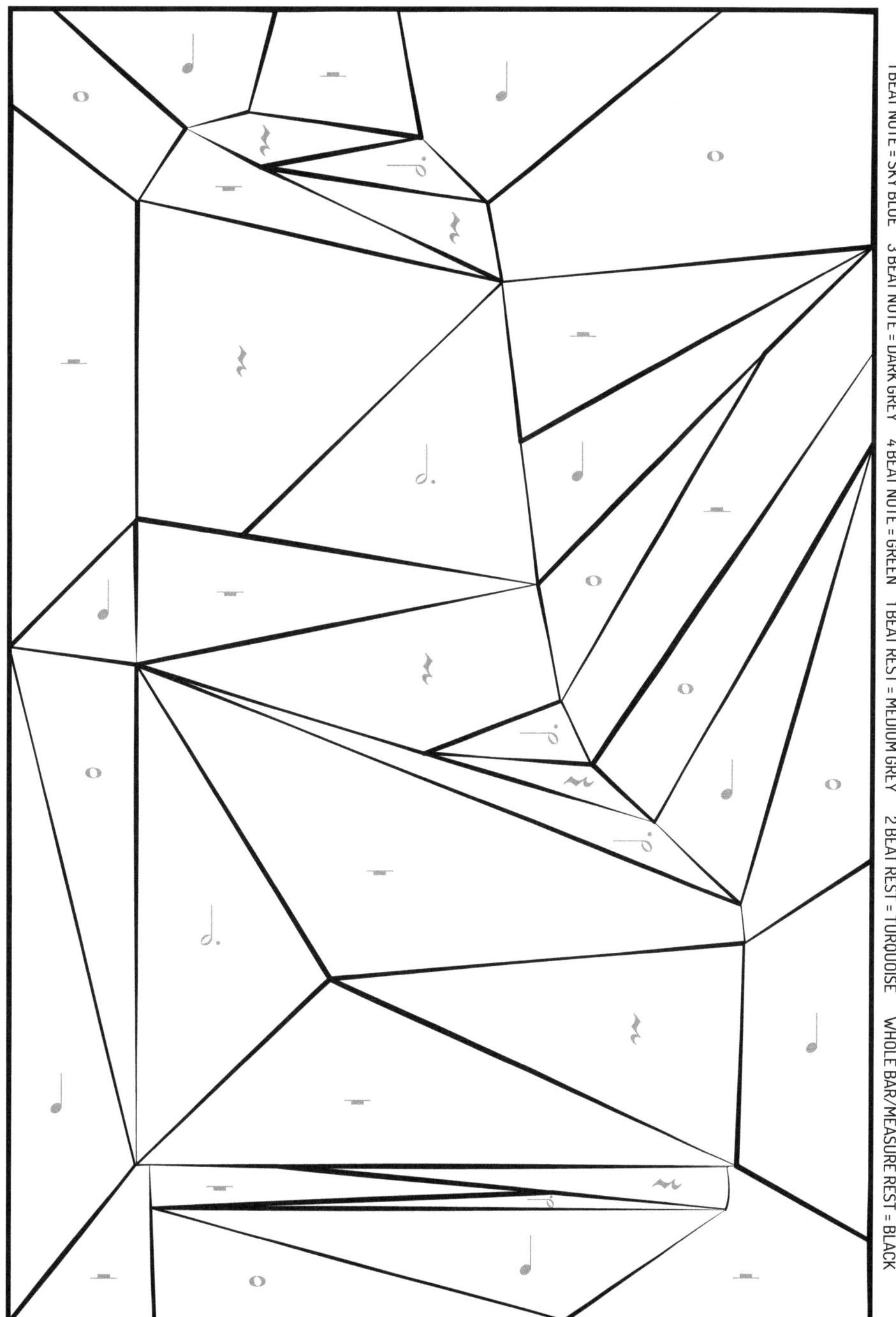

VERY LOUD=MEDIUM PURPLE   LOUD=DARK PURPLE   MODERATELY LOUD=MAROON   MODERATELY SOFT=LIGHT ORANGE   SOFT=CREAM   VERY SOFT=YELLOW

© Copyright Colourful Keys 2018
www.vibrantmusicteaching.com

GETTING SLOWER=DARK GREY   GRADUALLY GETTING LOUDER=MEDIUM BROWN   BACK TO ORIGINAL TEMPO=PALE PINK   GETTING FASTER=BRIGHT PINK   GRADUALLY GETTING SOFTER=LILAC

© Copyright Colourful Keys 2018
www.vibrantmusicteaching.com

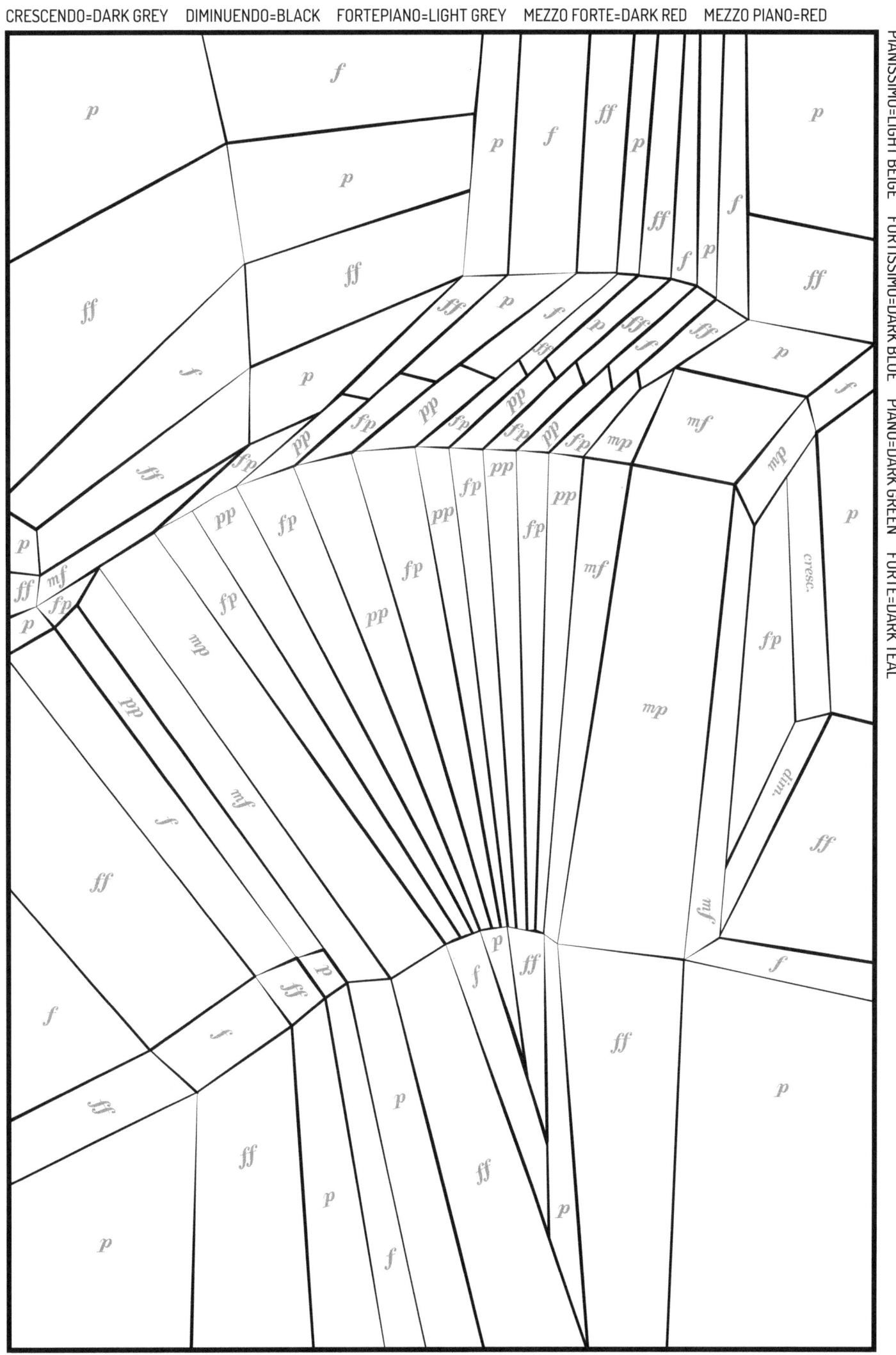

GRADUALLY GETTING LOUDER=YELLOW   GETTING SLOWER=SKY BLUE   GETTING A LITTLE SLOWER=MEDIUM BLUE

REPEAT=BLUE-GREEN   GRADUALLY GETTING SOFTER=ORANGE   ONE OCTAVE HIGHER=LIGHT BROWN

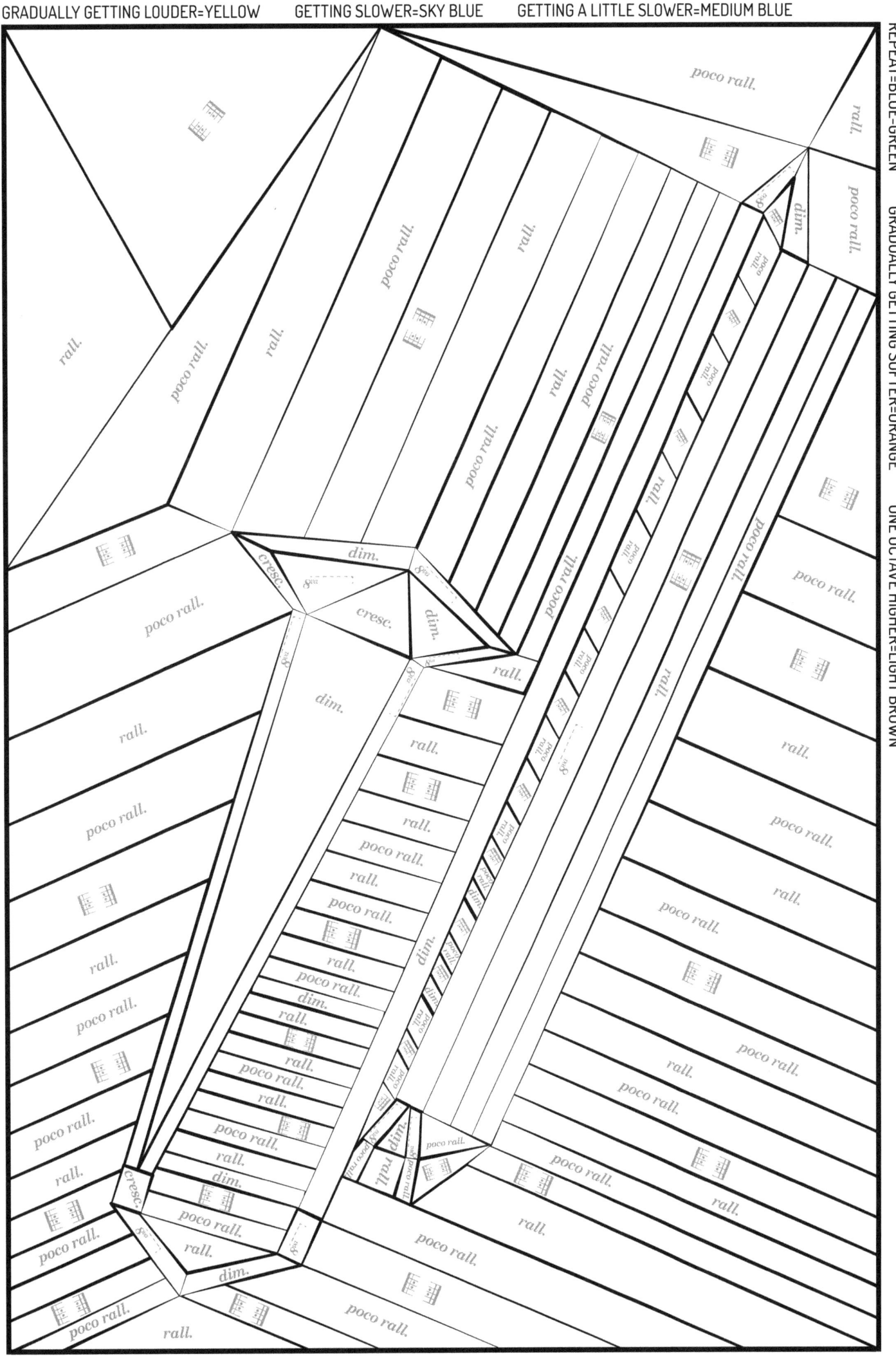

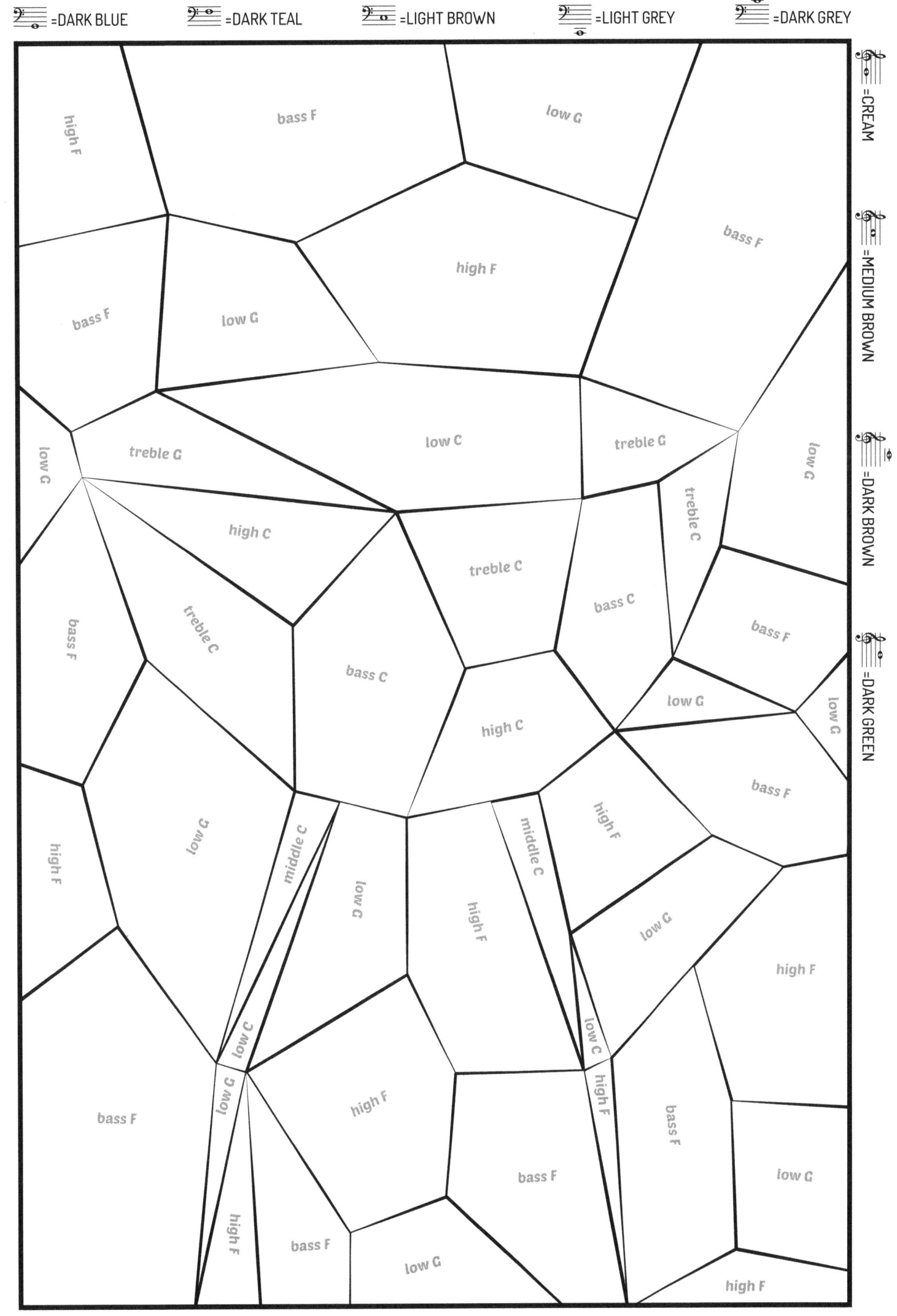

LIVELY=RED GRADUALLY GETTING LOUDER=GREEN GRADUALLY GETTING SOFTER=YELLOW PLAYFULLY=BLUE

GRACEFULLY=MEDIUM BROWN
ALWAYS LOUD=LIGHT BROWN
EXPRESSIVELY=LIGHT GREY
ALWAYS SOFT=PALE YELLOW
MAJESTICALLY=CREAM

9TH=YELLOW   7TH=DARK GREY   5TH=MEDIUM GREEN   3RD=MEDIUM BROWN   2ND=DARK BROWN   4TH=LIGHT BROWN   6TH=DARK GREEN   8VE=LIGHT GREEN

© Copyright Colourful Keys 2018
www.vibrantmusicteaching.com

WALKING PACE=DARK GREEN   MODERATE SPEED=MEDIUM GREEN   2ND ENDING=LIGHT GREEN   1ST ENDING=YELLOW   MODERATELY QUICK=PALE ORANGE   GETTING SLOWER=ORANGE

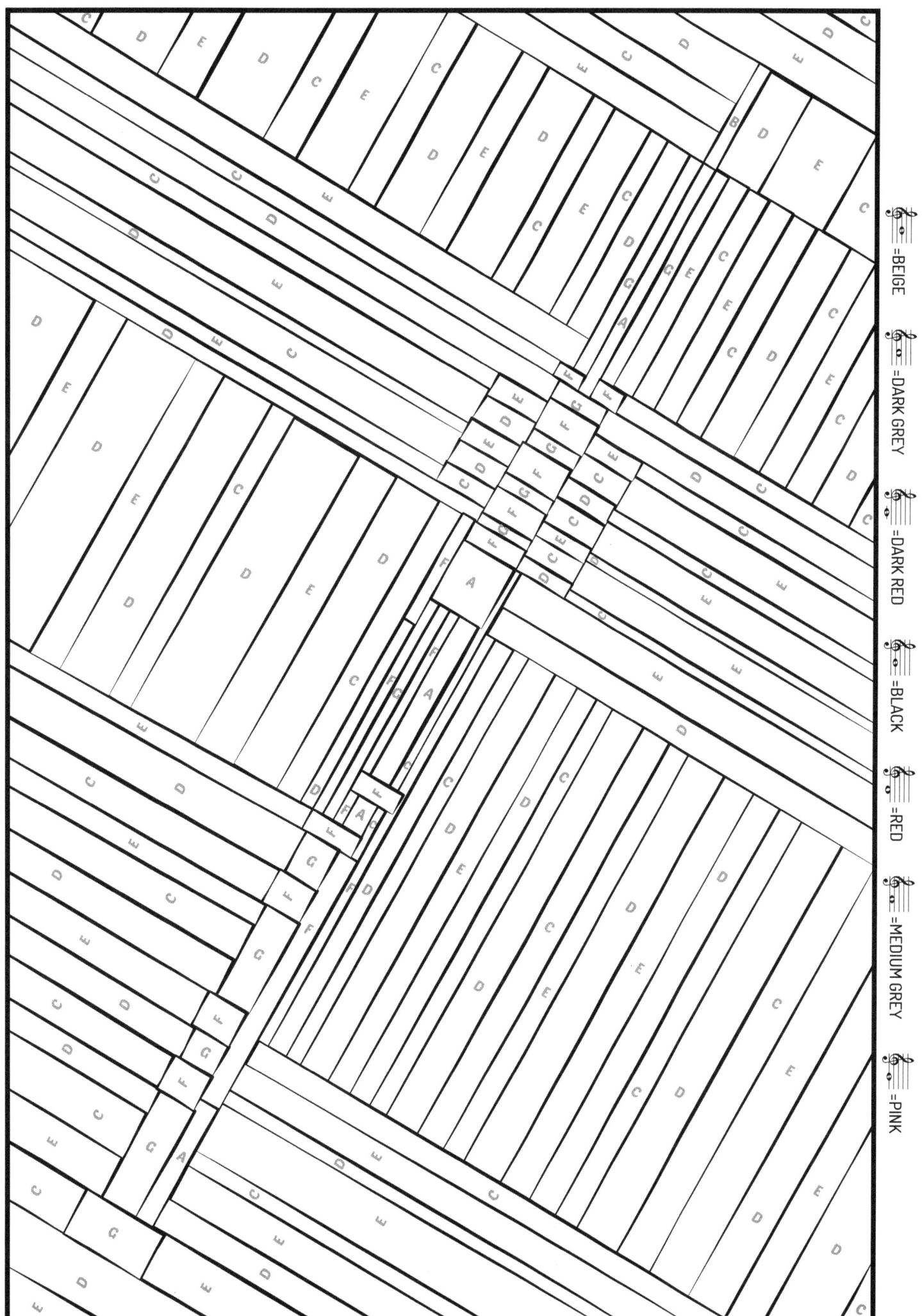

SIMPLE QUADRUPLE TIME=BLACK   SIMPLE TRIPLE TIME=DARK GREY   CUT COMMON TIME=MEDIUM GREY   TRIPLET=LIGHT BROWN

COMMON TIME=LIGHT GREY   COMPOUND TRIPLE TIME=BEIGE   SIMPLE DUPLE TIME=LIGHT GREEN   COMPOUND DUPLE TIME=MEDIUM GREEN   COMPOUND QUADRUPLE TIME=DARK GREEN

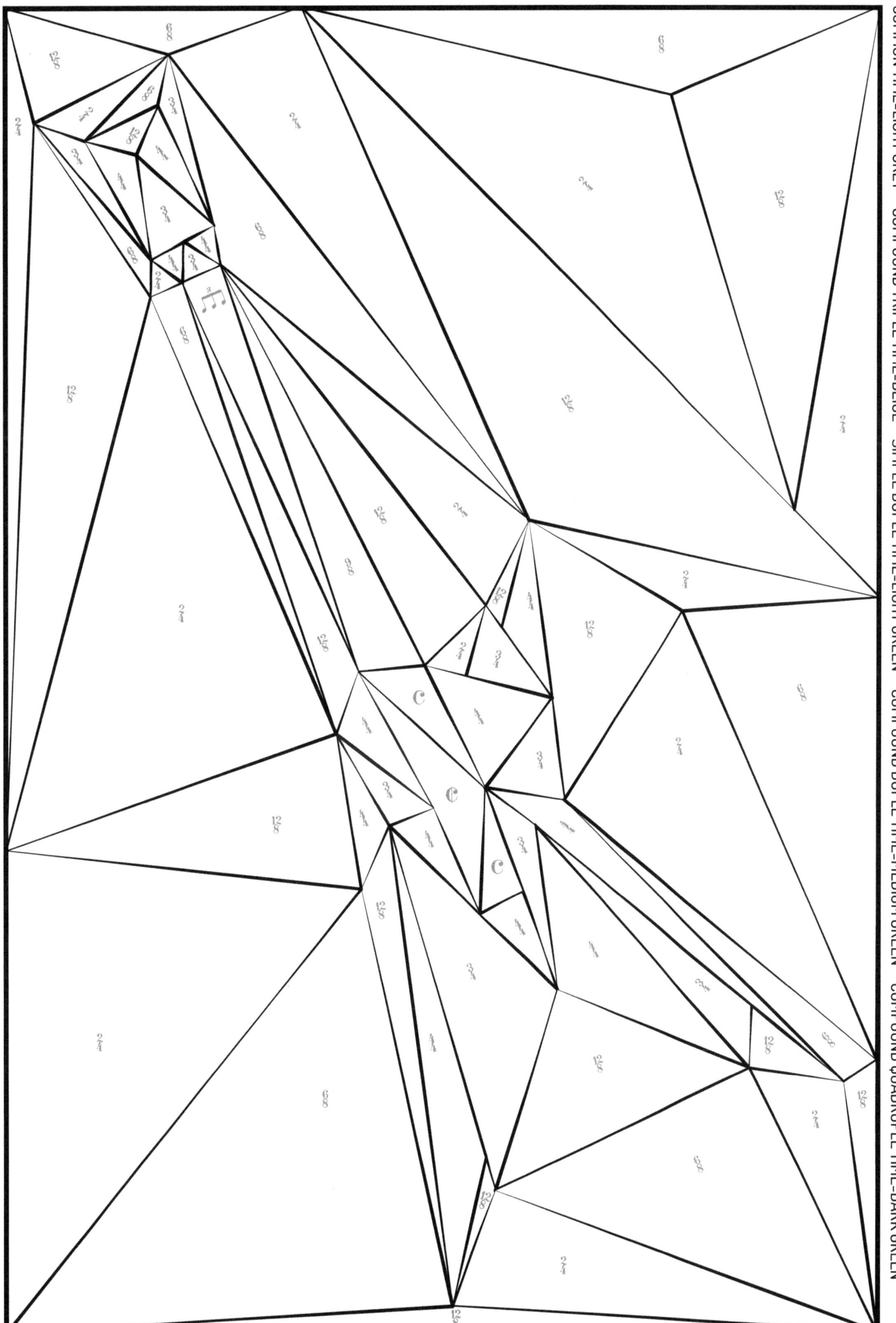

© Copyright Colourful Keys 2018
www.vibrantmusicteaching.com

FAST=CREAM   QUICK & LIVELY=LIGHT BROWN   SLOW=MEDIUM BROWN   WALKING PACE=BLUE   LIKE A MARCH=GREEN   MODERATE SPEED=BLUE-GREEN

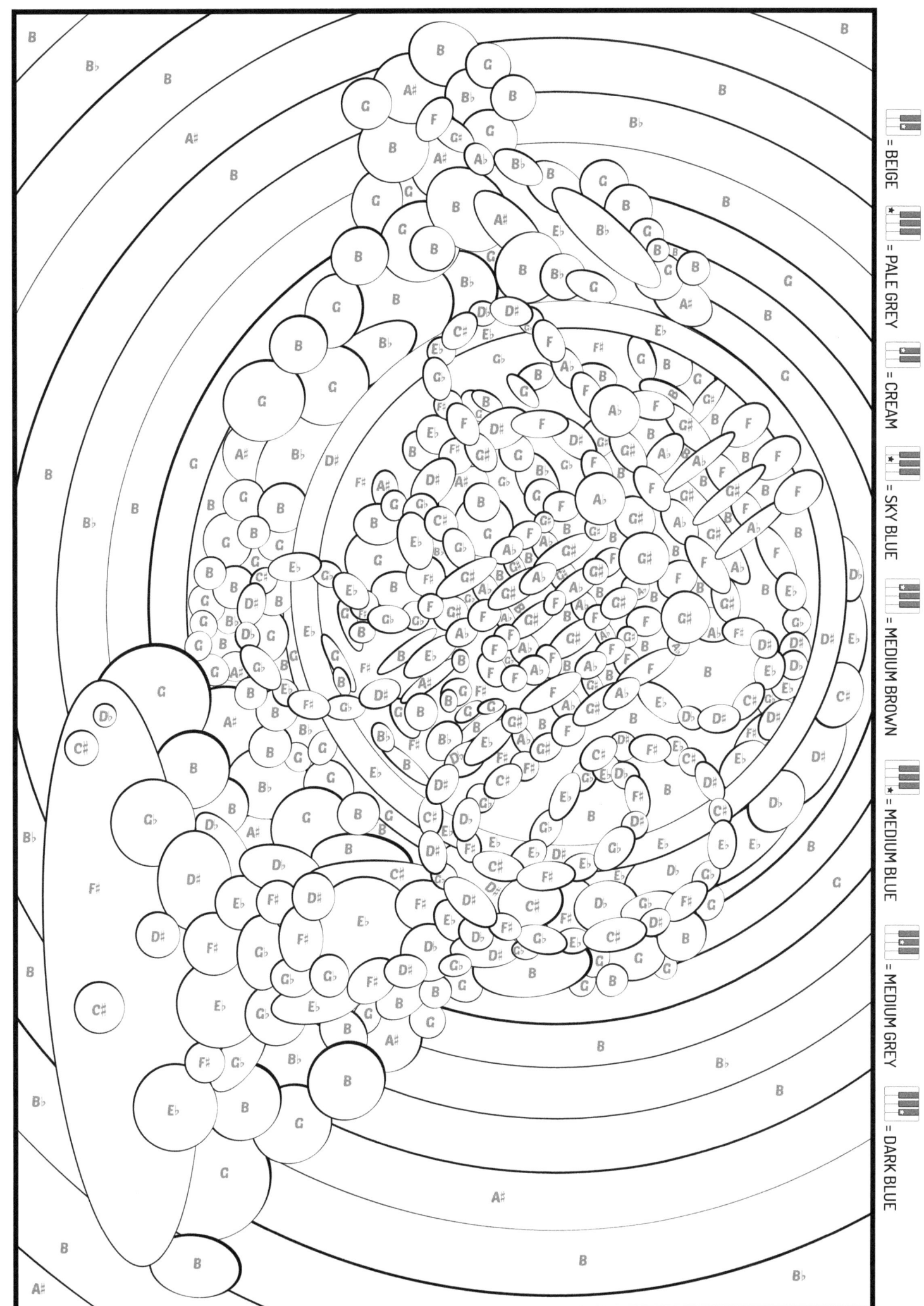

SHARP=MAROON   FLAT=DARK PURPLE   NATURAL=MEDIUM PURPLE   MARCATO=BLACK   TENUTO=DARK BROWN   STACCATO=MEDIUM BROWN   ACCENT=LIGHT BROWN   FERMATA=DARK GREY

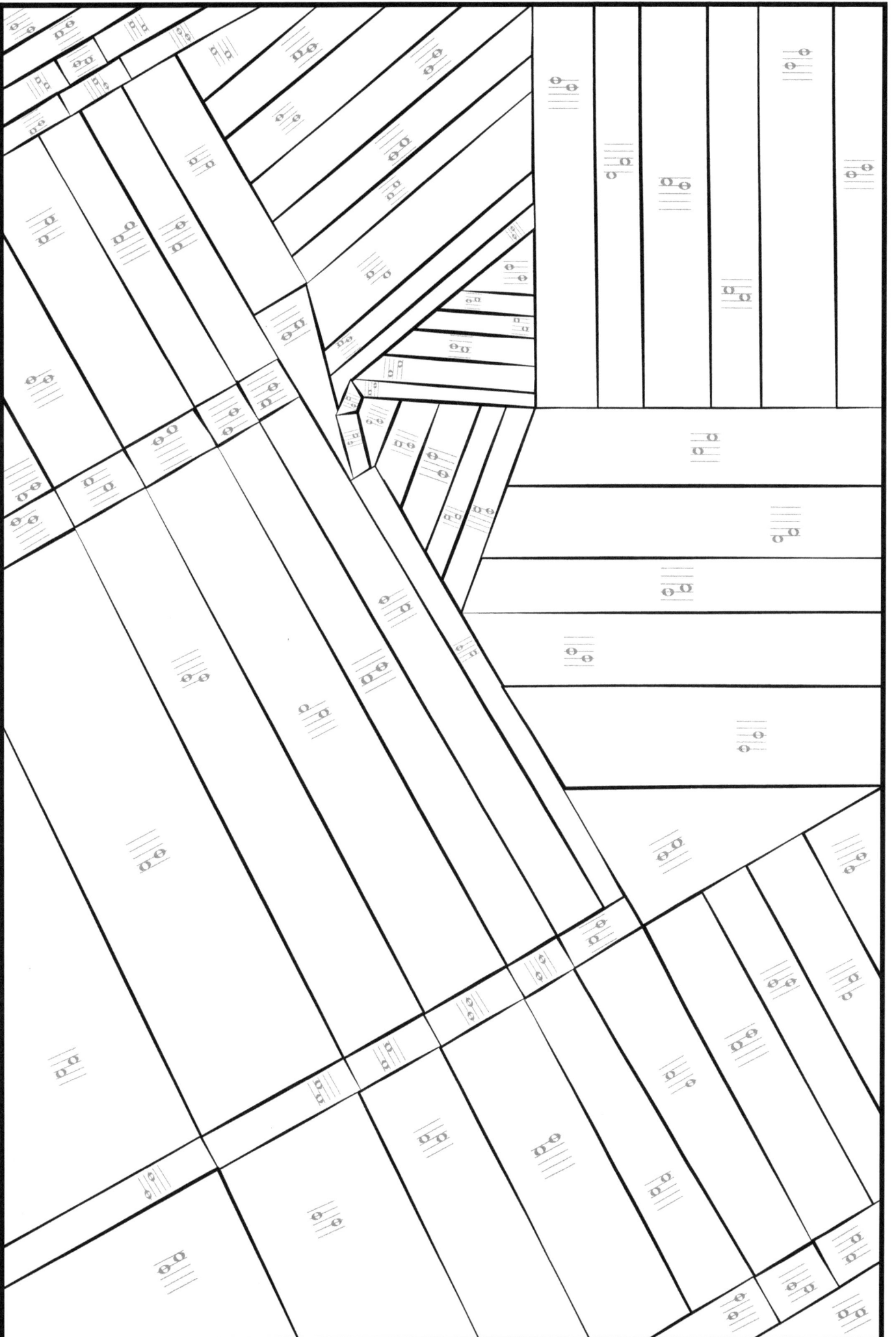

COMMON TIME=BLACK   CUT COMMON TIME=CREAM   ¼ BEAT REST=LIGHT GREY   ½ BEAT REST=DARK GREY   1 BEAT REST=BEIGE

2 BEAT REST=DARK BROWN   2 BEATS IN A BAR/MEASURE=DARK PURPLE   3 BEATS IN A BAR/MEASURE=DARK BLUE   4 BEATS IN A BAR/MEASURE=MEDIUM PURPLE

© Copyright Colourful Keys 2018
www.vibrantmusicteaching.com

LESS MOVEMENT=VERY PALE GREY   MORE MOVEMENT=MEDIUM GREY   ORIGINAL SPEED=LIGHT GREY

GETTING SLOWER=DARK GREY

GETTING SOFTER=MAROON

WITH MOVEMENT=PURPLE

GETTING FASTER=DARK PURPLE

CPSIA information can be obtained
at www.ICGtesting.com
Printed in the USA
BVHW050352210819
556220BV00046BA/2708/P